THE BUILDER

Anne Civardi
Illustrated by Stephen Cartwright

Designed by Roger Priddy

Reading Consultant: Betty Root
Reading and Language Information Centre
Reading University, England.

BERT

OSCAR

HARRY HAMMER

SID CEMENT

SALLY SPARK

TERRY TILE

POLLY FILLER

MATT BRUSH

THE BUILDER

THE CARPENTER

THE BRICK LAYER

THE ELECTRICIAN

THE TILER

THE PLASTERER

THE PAINTER

Bert Brick is a builder.
His dog is called Oscar.

Bert is going to do some
building for Mr. Short.

He wants a new room
built on to his house.

Bert tells Mr. Short how
much the job will cost.

2

He shows the plans to Sid, Harry and Terry.
They are going to help Bert build the new room.

The next day, Bert goes to
Mr. Short's house.

He drives off in his
new pick-up truck.

Bert stops the truck
outside the front gate.

He carries his big
ladder to the house.

He meets Mrs. Short, Jack, Rosie, Tuff and Paws.
Mrs. Short is going to have a baby soon.

4

Bert climbs up his ladder on to the garage roof.
He is going to build a bedroom for the baby here.

5

He measures to see how big the bedroom will be.

Then he drives off to the builder's yard.

Bert orders cement, wood, bricks and tiles.

And lots of paint, nails, plaster and screws.

Bert will take some of the things in his truck.
Joe Tool will deliver the rest in the morning.

Joe tells his workers to load up the truck.
It is hard work, but they are strong and tough.

The next day, Bert starts work at the Shorts' house.
Sid, Harry and Terry have come to help him.

They put up scaffolding
beside the garage.

Then Bert helps Joe Tool
unload his truck.

Terry helps Harry pull the old roof off the garage.
Harry will lay a floor here for the new room.

9

The next day, Harry nails down big pieces of wood to hold the new floor. He is a very good carpenter.

10

Sid is the bricklayer. He builds the walls.

He mixes the mortar. It sticks bricks together.

Sid starts to lay the bricks for the walls.

But naughty Paws knocks over Sid's mortar.

It falls on Bert's head.
Jack thinks it is funny.

Poor Bert is very dirty.
He is cross with Paws.

Mrs. Short takes Bert into
the house to wash.

Sid chases away Paws.
He gets on with his work.

It takes him two days to build all the walls.

Then Harry fixes in the frames for the windows.

Now Bert, Sid and Harry start to build the roof. They nail together the big wooden rafters.

Terry, the tiler, puts felt over the rafters.

He nails on the roof tiles. But just look at Paws.

Bert knocks a hole for a door into the room.

Mrs. Short helps to clean up the mess.

It is nearly time for her to have her baby.

Mr. Short drives her off to the hospital.

Now Bert helps Harry lay the new floor. They nail down lots of long wooden floorboards.

Now Sally Spark, the electrician, starts work.

She marks where to put the plugs and switches.

And she drills holes in the wood for the cables.

Jack wants to help Sally, but Rosie wants to play.

She knocks Sally off her step-ladder.

Bert helps poor Sally to get up.

Just then, Mr. Short comes home from the hospital. Mrs. Short has had a new baby boy.

The next day, Polly, the plasterer, starts work.

Bert helps her to put up a new ceiling.

Polly mixes up lots of new plaster.

18

She puts it all over the brick walls.

Oscar chases Tuff and knocks over the plaster.

It falls on the floor. Polly mixes some more.

She finishes the walls. Harry hangs the door.
Bert fixes glass into all the windows.

When the plaster is dry, Matt, the painter, begins.

He and Bert sandpaper the woodwork and walls.

Matt paints the ceiling with a long roller.

He does not see Paws get into his paintpot.

20

Now she is covered with paint.

Matt cuts and pastes pieces of wallpaper.

He sticks them to the walls of the room.

He works very hard. The room is soon finished.

The next day, Fred comes to lay a new carpet.

Sally and Bert carry a cot into the bedroom.

Sid and Polly get the room clean and tidy.
Mr. Short goes off to fetch the new baby.

Jack and Rosie come home with their baby brother.

They all go upstairs to look at his bedroom.

Bert and his workmates are waiting to see him. Mrs. Short is very pleased with their work.

Now it is time for Bert and his builders to leave.
They have done a good job for Mr. and Mrs. Short.

First published in 1986. Usborne Publishing Ltd, 20 Garrick Street, London WC2E 9BJ, England. © Usborne Publishing Ltd, 1986.